RUBANK EDUCATIONAL LIBRARY No. 89

RUBANK *M* INTERMEDIATE *Method*

OBOE

J. E. SKORNICKA and R. KOEBNER

A FOLLOW UP COURSE FOR INDIVIDUAL
OR LIKE-INSTRUMENT CLASS INSTRUCTION

RUBANK®

HAL•LEONARD
CORPORATION
7777 W. Bluemound Rd. P.O. Box 13819 Milwaukee, WI 53213

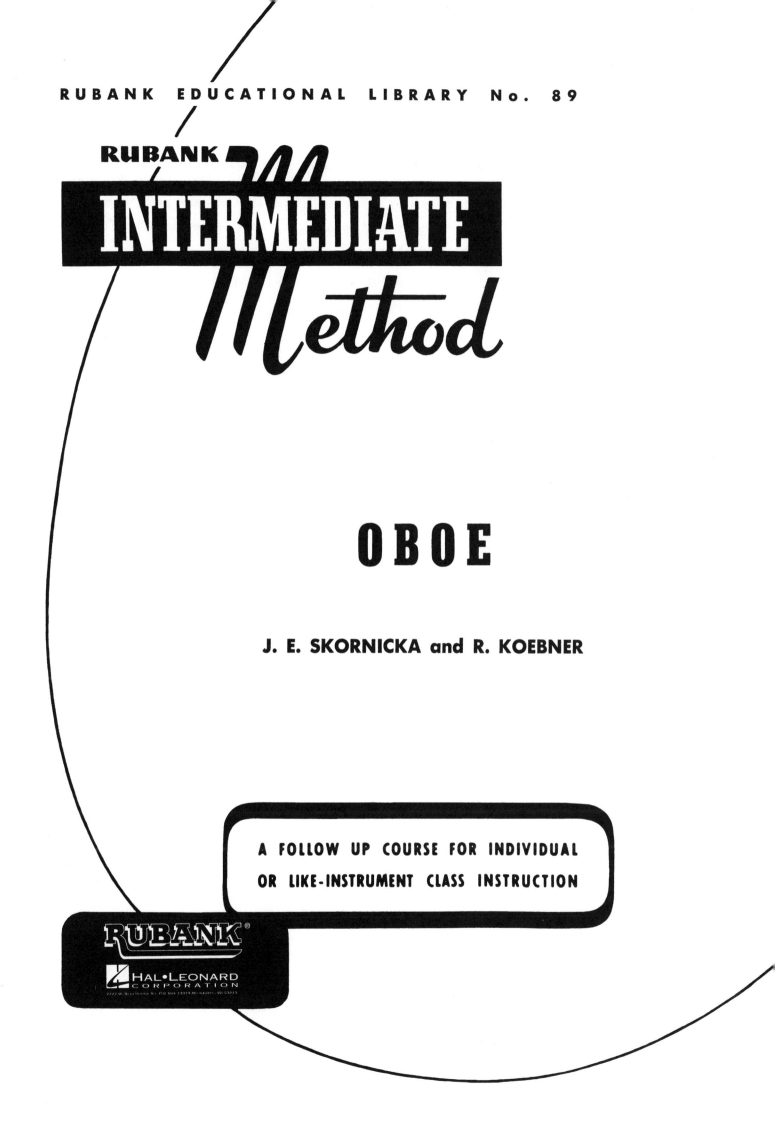

ESSENTIAL PRINCIPLES
of
Good Instrumental Performance

GOOD TONE is necessary in order that one's playing be pleasing to the listener as well as the player. Good tone can be produced only when the instrument is in good playing condition, equipped with the correct type of mouthpiece and played with the correct embouchure.

INTONATION: When two successive tones of different pitch are produced, it is necessary that each tone be in tune with the other, relative to the interval being played.

TUNE: The player must develop and train his ear so that a difference of pitch can be distinguished when playing with others.

NOTE VALUES: The player must develop a rhythmic sense so as to give proper value to tones as represented by the written notes.

BREATHING AND PHRASING: Each is usually dependent on the other. Since teachers of wind instruments differ on the methods of breathing, no special method is advocated, but it soon becomes evident to all players that in order to get good musical phrasing, it is necessary to breathe properly and in the proper places of a composition. It will be to the pupil's advantage to spend much time and effort on this phase of playing and take seriously all suggestions given by the teacher.

EXPRESSION MARKS: Expression marks in music are considered just as important as punctuation in prose and poetry. Good phrasing is the performance of music that has been properly punctuated. Expression marks put character into a mass of notes and if properly observed, will produce satisfying musical effects.

RELAXATION AND PROPER POSITION OF BODY AND HANDS: Whether playing in standing or sitting position, it is necessary that the body be erect and relaxed. Relaxation is the secret to the accomplishment of success in many other professions and trades. The arms must be relaxed, the elbows away from the body and the hands assuming a restful position on the instrument.

SUFFICIENT TIME FOR PRACTICE: Since different pupils require different types and lengths of practice periods, the objective that every pupil should establish is: "I will master the assigned task whether it takes 1/2 or 2 hours." The accomplishment of a task is far more important than the time that it consumes.

PROPER CARE OF THE INSTRUMENT: Carelessness in the handling of an instrument is the most prevalent handicap to the progress of young players. No pupil can expect to produce good results if the instrument is in poor playing condition. The instrument must be handled carefully and when a disorder is discovered, have it remedied immediately. Constant attention as to the condition of an instrument will pay dividends in the end.

MENTAL ATTITUDE OF TEACHER AND PUPIL: In order that the musical results be satisfactory, both the pupil and teacher must be interested in their task, and must have a perfect understanding of what that task is. The teacher must understand the learning capacities of the pupil so that the pupil in turn will get the type and amount of instruction that he will understand and be able to master.

J.E.S.

Review Lesson

1. The Oboe is essentially a "tone" instrument and its quality of tone lends itself especially to lyric passages in the finest of classic compositions.

   Special and serious consideration must be given to the attainment of a good tone, the most important factors being:

   a. An easy-blowing reed, (not too stiff nor too soft).

   b. Special attention to correct lip position. (lips firm around teeth and a smiling position of the mouth).

   c. As little pressure as possible on the reed, (to allow free reed vibration).Too much pressure on the reed is a serious common fault of the average player and considered one of the great handicaps to good tone production.

   d. Build the embouchure,(the position of the lips,) as near the tip as possible. The tip of the reed is the restricted playing area.

2. Tune carefully by checking the A or Bb with a tuning fork or a tuning bar. Feel free to adjust the reed, pushing it in or pulling it out of the socket to acquire the proper pitch.   This adjustment of the reed does not effect the quality of tone.

* The F indicated above is fingered with key "B;' or fork fingering. which is always used when the F is followed or preceded by either a D or an Eb. Similar references will be made to fingerings, all of which can be found and verified on the accompanying chart.

   Make a habit of referring to the chart for correct fingerings.

MARKS OF EXPRESSION AND THEIR USE

PIANISSIMO	pp	very soft		FORTISSIMO	ff	Very loud
PIANO	p	Soft		FORTE	f	Loud
MEZZO-PIANO	mp	Medium soft		MEZZO FORTE	mf	Medium loud

mf or mezzo forte is considered the normal tone on the Oboe.

In playing a tone on the Oboe, (unless otherwise marked) the tone should be held at the same level of volume, without increasing or diminishing the volume. This type of tone in the succeeding studies will be indicated by means of parallel lines, thus: ═══════

The distance between the parallel lines will indicate the comparative difference in volume to be used.

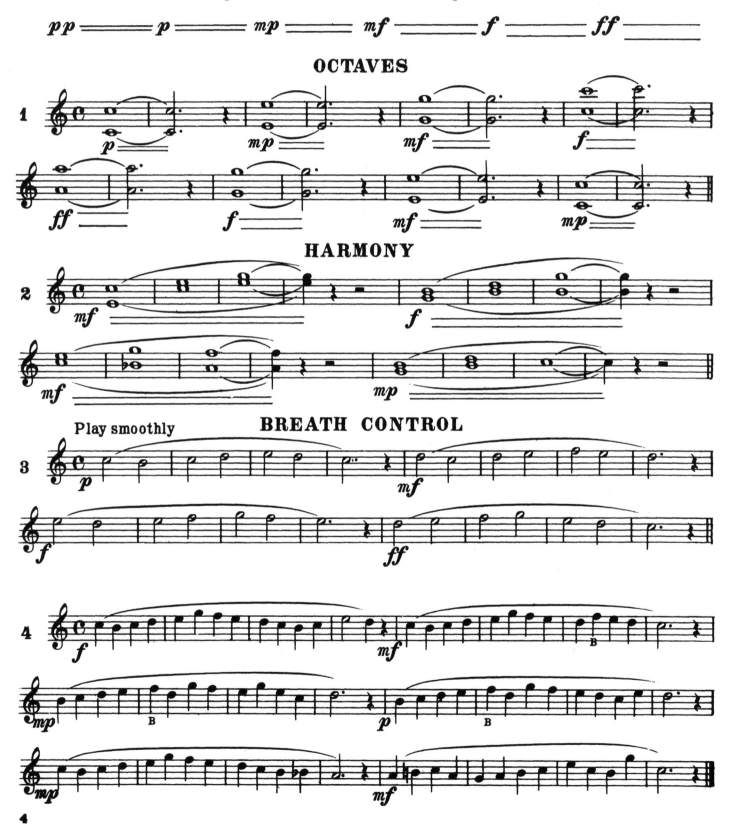

OCTAVES

HARMONY

BREATH CONTROL

Play smoothly

4

STUDIES IN EXPRESSION
Sound Graduations

Crescendo (cresc) Gradually louder.

Decrescendo (decresc) Gradually softer

Diminuendo (dim) Gradually softer

Crescendo and diminuendo must be gradual. The tone increases or decreases in volume gradually. In either case, the pitch of the tone or tones must not be altered. Study the correct and incorrect examples below.

STUDIES IN ACCENTS AND EXPRESSION MARKS

The ACCENT (>) (rinforzando) is placed over or under the note which is to receive special emphasis. In order to make such a note predominant with the least amount of effort, it is usually advisable to play the notes before and after the accented tone softer and shorter. This contrast alone produces the desired effect without overemphasizing the accented note.

MELODY

WOODEN SHOE DANCE

PETITE GAVOTTE

R. K.

ARTICULATION AND EXPRESSION

Play the above study with each of the following articulations. (Observe accents)

DAILY STUDIES FOR THE DEVELOPMENT OF TECHNIC

The studies on this page are intended for daily home practice.

Play each study with a steady tempo, slowly at first, but increase the tempo each day until every study on this page can be played Allegro.

Legato Duet

9

Staccato Studies

1. Utmost caution must be exercised in avoiding an "edge" on the end of a tone in the production of a staccato. Do not stop the tone with a "t" or the tongue, in the attempt to play the note short. The tongue must be drawn back quickly from the tip of the reed when starting the tone and must remain back until the next tone is to be started. The tone is terminated by the arrest of the air column and a slight bounce of the lips, namely, Ta-Ta-Ta and not Tut-Tut-Tut.

2. Use one tone in repetition for best staccato development.

3. Practice the staccato slowly and very short until you get perfect symmetry as to duration, pitch, and quality of each tone.

EXCERPTS FROM SURPRISE SYMPHONY

HAYDN

ETUDE IN A MINOR

F Major Studies

STACCATO ETUDE

D MINOR SCALES

✳ Always play C♯ as indicated on the fingering chart

ETUDE IN D MINOR

ETUDE

ARTICULATION ETUDE

BARRET

BOHEMIAN FOLK SONG

LULLABY

BRAHMS

B♭ Major Studies

1 Chord

2 Scale

ETUDE

3 Moderato
mf

JIG-SAW

R.K.

4 *mf*

NOTE: As you increase the tempo of the above exercise, also slur 2 measures at a time, then 4 measures, then the 8 measures.

G MINOR SCALES

Harmonic   Melodic

Daily Study

HUNTING HORNS

R.K.

BOHEMIAN LULLABY

Excerpt from Masaniello Overture - AUBER

G Major Studies

SALUT d'AMOUR

ELGAR

E MINOR SCALES

Legato Etude

TECHNIC DEVELOPMENT

DUET IN E MINOR

R.K.

Syncopation

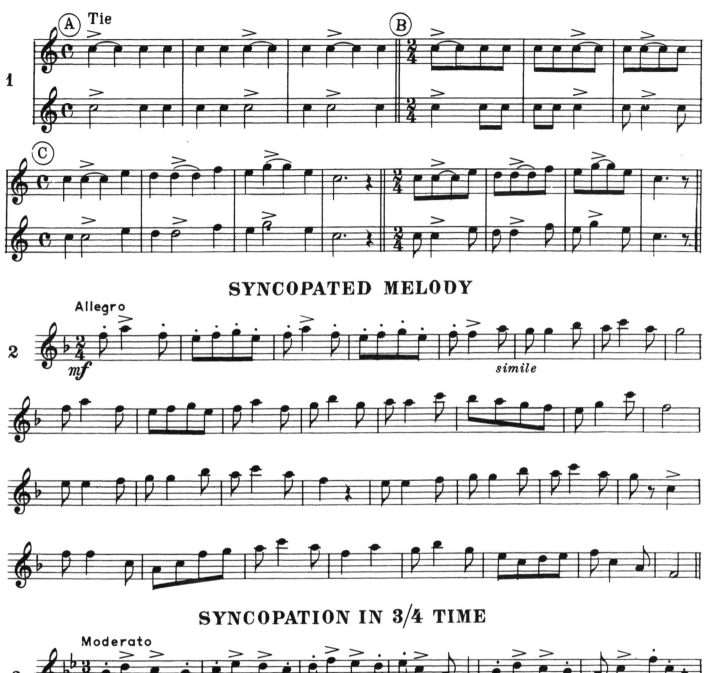

SYNCOPATED MELODY

SYNCOPATION IN 3/4 TIME

CHORD STUDY

Eb Major Studies

TECHNICAL ETUDE

C MINOR SCALES

Oriental Dusk

R.K.

CRUSADERS HYMN

Traditional

6/8 Rhythm

PETITE MARCH

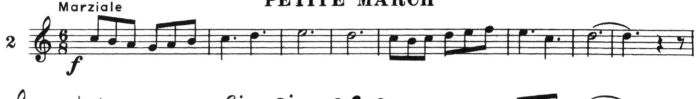

POP GOES THE WEASEL

Folk Tune

DRINK TO ME ONLY WITH THINE EYES

Old English

ETUDE

20

D Major Studies

Chord

1

Scale

2

PRAYER

R.K.

Moderato

3

B MINOR SCALES

Harmonic ... **Melodic**

4

16th Note Rhythm Studies

SCALE ETUDE

Play the above etude with each of the following articulations.

RHYTHMIC PATTERNS FOR DAILY STUDY

A♭ Major Studies

Chord

1

Scale

2

USING KEY 4

3

DUET

4

F MINOR SCALES

Harmonic   **Melodic**

Excerpt from Symphony No.7

SCHUBERT

NEW WORLD SYMPHONY

DVORAK

Hold down
Keys 4 and 3
throughout measure

DUET

J. S. BACH

Dotted Eighth Note Studies

1

STACCATO ETUDE

2

DUET

HAYDN-BRAHMS

3

Folk Dance

EXCERPT FROM MEISTERSINGER OVERTURE

WAGNER

TRAMP! TRAMP! TRAMP!

ROOT

D.S. al Fine

Triplet Studies

Similarity between 6/8 and 2/4 tempo when the Triplet is used

1

ETUDE IN B MINOR

Allegro

2

SERENADE

R. K.

3

EXCERPT FROM OBERON

VON WEBER

Allegro molto

4

(*) An extra dot always adds half the value of the preceding dot to the note.

LAMENT

Andantino

5

A Major Studies

1 Chord

2 Scale

EXCERPT FROM CAPRICCIO ITALIEN

TSCHAIKOWSKY

3 Allegretto

EXCERPT FROM 7th SYMPHONY

BEETHOVEN

4 Allegro

F# MINOR SCALES

5 Harmonic   Melodic

Duet in 6/8

Chromatic Studies

R.K.

30

Grace Notes

There are two kinds of single grace notes, SHORT and LONG. The long grace note assumes 1/2 the length of the note which it precedes. It is seldom used since it is more practical to write out the two notes of equal length. *The Short Grace Note* is the one most commonly used. It may be played either before or on the beat, just as the composition may require. There are also *Double and Triple Grace Notes* which are played quickly either on or before the beat, this also being determined by the type of composition being played.

NOTE: It is deemed advisable to play the grace notes with the regular fingerings. Consult the Trill Chart, however, when substitute fingerings are of vital importance in the execution of difficult grace note passages.

31

ETUDE IN DOUDLE GRACE NOTES

EXCERPT FROM SYMPHONY No. 7

SCHUBERT

EXCERPT FROM MARCH SLAV

TSCHAIKOWSKY

EXCERPT FROM POLOVETZIAN DANCES

BORODIN

PROCESSIONAL

R. K.

Trills

A Trill is produced by alternating the given or written tone and the next scale tone above in rapid succession. As an example, if the given or written tone to be trilled is E with C major as the key, the scale tone above will be F natural. If, however, the key being played is G major, the next scale tone above E will be F♯. In the first instance, the trill will alternate between E and F natural and in the second instance, between E and F♯.

The approximate number of notes usually played on a trilled tone is shown below:

If it is intended that the upper note of the trill should be either a half tone higher or lower than required by the signature, such change is shown by an accidental placed above the sign of the trill, thus:

In order to finish a trill more elegantly, grace notes (to be played leisurely) are added, thus:

An exception to the approximate number of notes comprising the trill as shown at the top of the page is sometimes made (in accordance with good musical judgement) in slow solo passages or cadenzas, for example:

Many trills require special fingerings which only your trill chart will indicate. Consult it frequently.

Trill Etudes

R. K.

Moderato

1

Moderato

R. K.

2

Andante

R. K.

3

DUET

Andante

R. K.

4

SHARPSHOOTERS' MARCH

METALO

Abbreviations

ABBREVIATION STUDIES

THERES MUSIC IN THE AIR

E Major Studies

Chords

Scale

In Thirds

THEN YOU'LL REMEMBER ME

Andante

Technical Etude

POLONAISE IN F♯ MINOR

R.K.

EXCERPT FROM 6th SYMPHONY

BEETHOVEN

EXCERPT FROM MANFRED OVERTURE

SCHUMANN

D♭ Major Studies

Chords

1 *staccato*

Scale

2

EXCERPT FROM SYMPHONY No. 4

TSCHAIKOWSKY

3 Andantino

EXCERPT FROM ROMEO AND JULIET OVERTURE

TSCHAIKOWSKY

4 ✱ Allegro moderato

B♭ MINOR SCALES

Harmonic

Melodic

✱ By using as little pressure as possible, and expanding the mouth to the utmost you can include this high register as part of your "big tone area."

The Gruppetto or Turn

Is composed of four grace notes following a principal note. The turn is designated by the following sign: ∾ A small sharp placed under this sign indicates that the lowest of the grace notes is sharpened; whereas if a sharp is placed above the sign, the upper grace note is sharpened. The same rule applies to flats, only that the aforementioned grace notes would be lowered a half tone.

The grace notes constituting the turn are played evenly except when the preceding principal note is dotted. In the following example illustrating this type, note carefully what happens to the last grace note.

After practicing the above measures separately, play them in succession.

ETUDE

R. K.

SERENADE

Key of B Major

Three Symphonic Excerpts

POLKA

J. E. S.

Trio for Oboes

J. S. BACH

Complete Trill Chart for the Conservatory System Oboe

Section Y shows finger placement for beginning the Trill.   Refer to fingering chart for symbols used.
Section Z shows the keys to be put in to motion to complete the Trill. (Fingering chart symbols used.)
Half-step trills are shown in the first column while whole-step trills are pictured in the last column of each section.

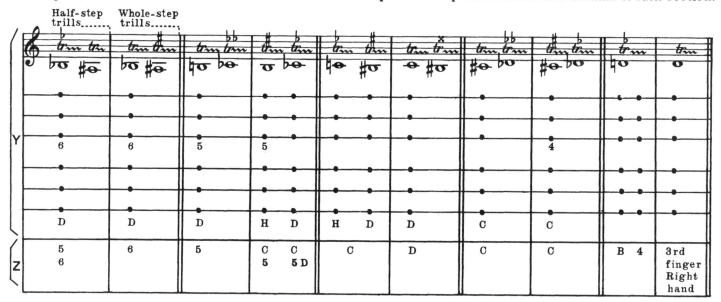

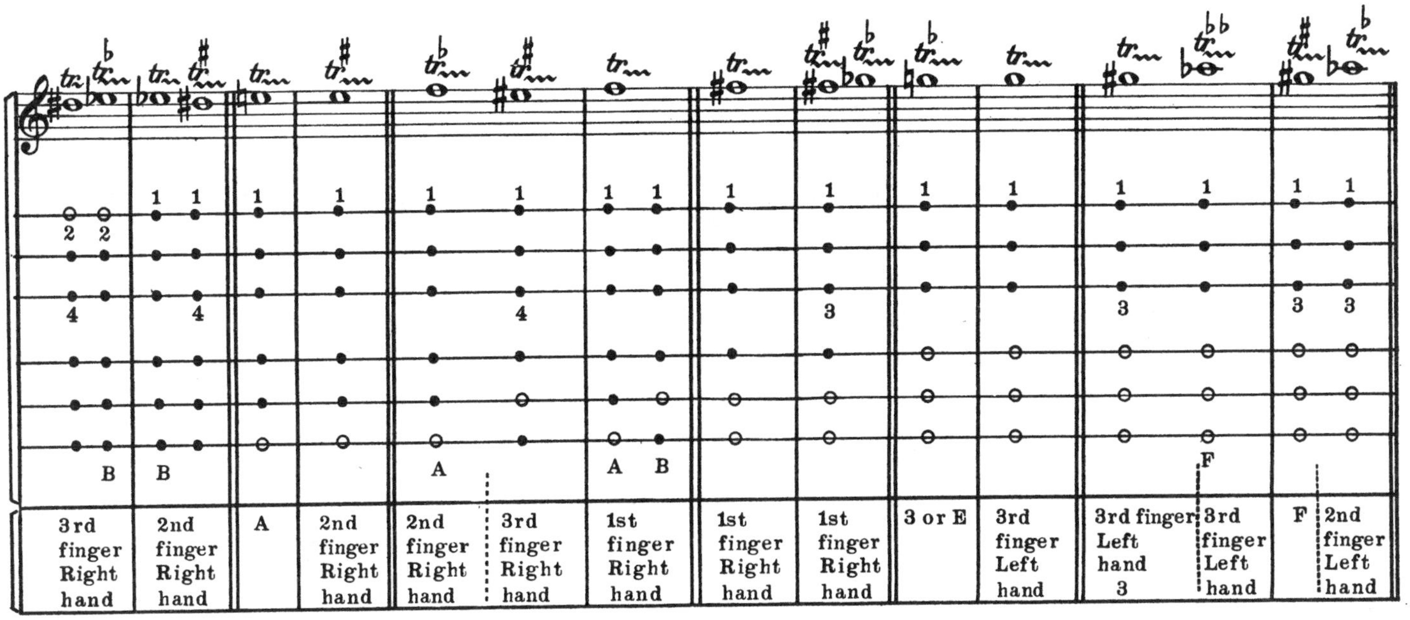
3rd finger Right hand
2nd finger Right hand
A
2nd finger Right hand
2nd finger Right hand
3rd finger Right hand
1st finger Right hand
1st finger Right hand
1st finger Right hand
3 or E
3rd finger Left hand
3rd finger Left hand 3
3rd finger Left hand
F
2nd finger Left hand

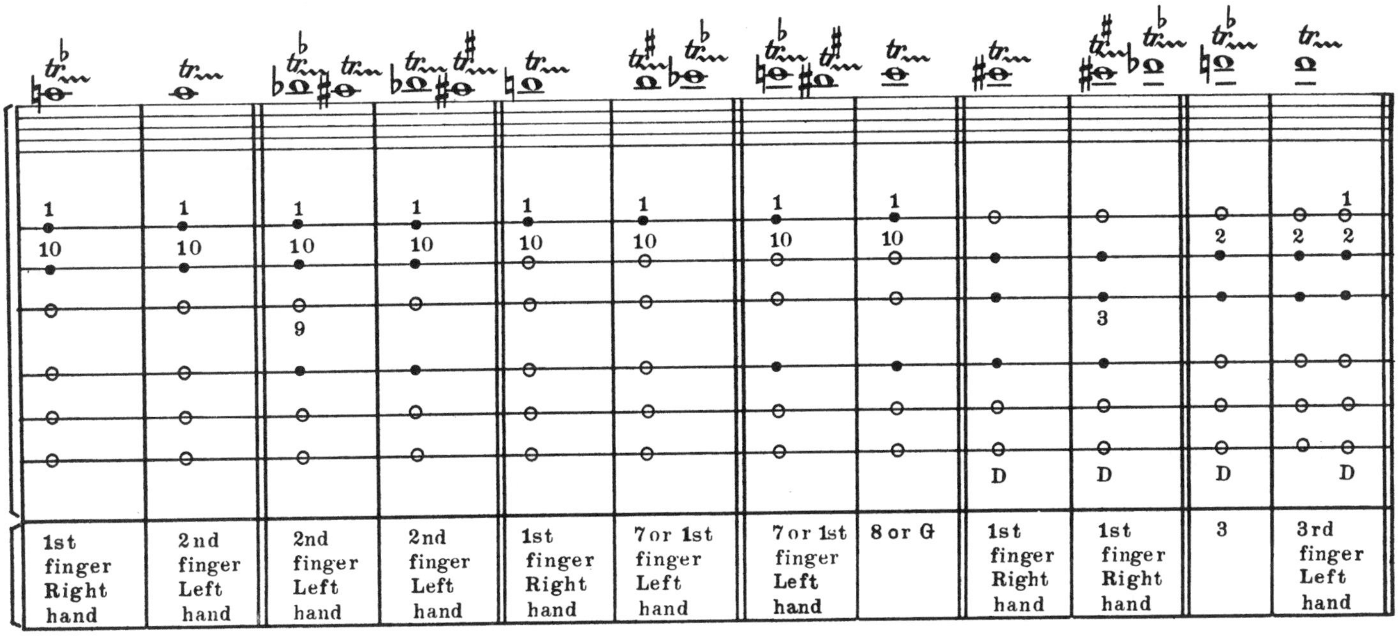
1st finger Right hand
2nd finger Left hand
2nd finger Left hand
2nd finger Left hand
1st finger Right hand
7 or 1st finger Left hand
7 or 1st finger Left hand
8 or G
1st finger Right hand
1st finger Right hand
3
3rd finger Left hand

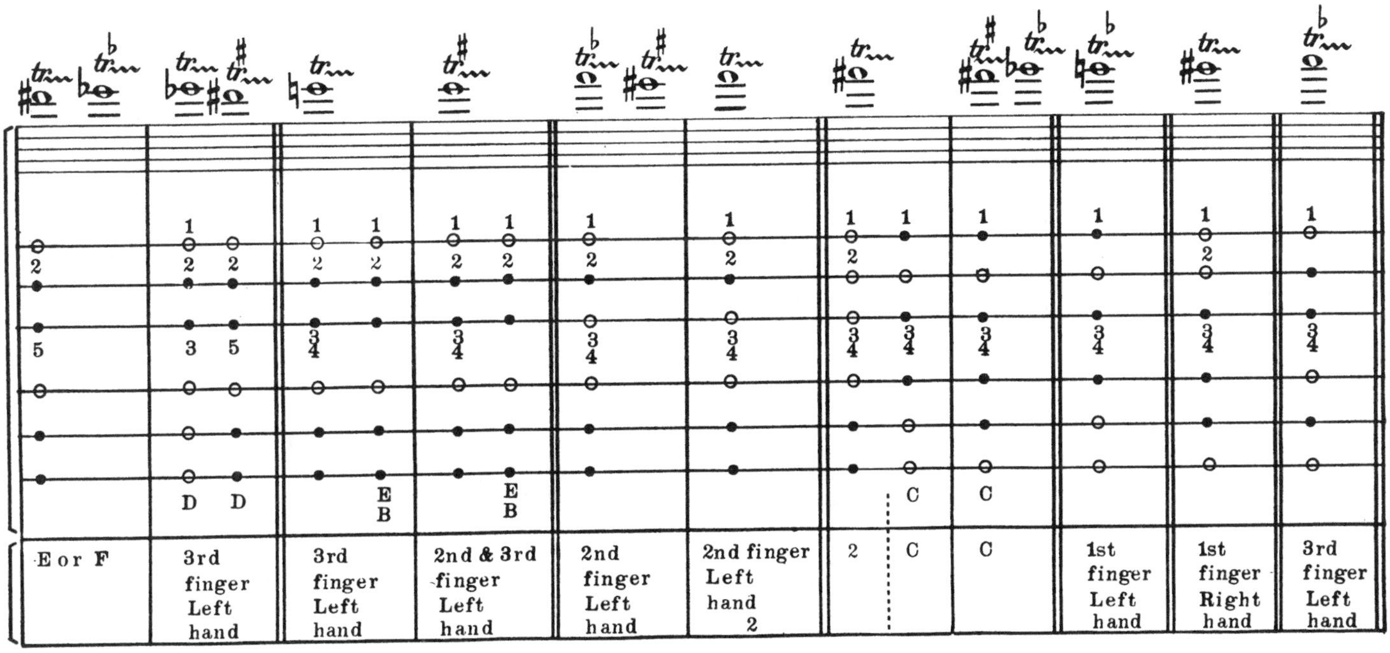
E or F
3rd finger Left hand
3rd finger Left hand
2nd & 3rd finger Left hand
2nd finger Left hand
2nd finger Left hand 2
2
C
C
1st finger Left hand
1st finger Right hand
3rd finger Left hand

Sonata

CORELLI